Death Dance of a Butterfly

Death Dance
of a Butterfly

Melba Joyce Boyd

Past Tents Press • Ferndale Michigan

Past Tents Press
332 W. Woodland
Ferndale MI. 48220- 2755
www. pasttentspress.com

Poems previously published: "Rearranging Your Father's Table," *Souls: A Critical Journal of Black Politics, Culture, and Society (2011)*; "Why I Observe the Sabbath at Home in the D," *Konch (2011)*; "Crystallizing the Moon," *Wayne Review (2011)*; "Bloodhounds on My Trail: Ode to Kathryne," *Amistad: Journal of African American Literature and Culture (2011)*; "Working It Out" and "A Walden Within Us," *Against the Current (2009)*; "Eulogy for Julia C. Collins," *African American Review (2006)*; "A Black Iron Pot," *The Black Scholar: Journal of Black Studies and Research(2006)*; "Miss Odessa" and "By Self Election-L'Raison d'Etre," *13th Moon: A Feminist Literary Magazine (2006)*; "Stage: Black," *Drumvoices Revue: A Confluence of Literary, Cultural & Vision Arts (2006)*; "Dancing is Flying," *A Broadside Annual (2005)*; "A Hand Painted Desert,"*Collegium for African American Research Newsletter (2005)*; "No One is Innocent, But" and "Poets in Pluto's Republic," *Dispatch Detroit (2003)*; "We Want Our City Back," *Abandon Automobile: Detroit City Poetry 2001 (2001)* and *The Black Scholar: Journal of Black Studies and Research (1994)*.

"Maple Red: a poetic interlude with the painting by Edward Clark" appears beneath the painting in the Detroit Institute of Arts, Detroit, 2008. "C'est une Histoire Extraordinaire" was originally published as a broadside for a memorial tribute for Prof. Michel Fabre at the University of Paris, France, 2008. "Phoenix Rising" was originally published as a limited edition broadside for the Coleman A. Young Foundation, Twenty-Fifth Anniversary Celebration, 2007. Lines from "We Want Our City Back" appear in the sculpture, *Transcending: Michigan Tribute to Labor* by Michael Hall and Sergio DeGuisti, installed in Hart Plaza, Detroit, Michigan, 2003.

Printed on acid free paper by Cushing- Malloy, Inc.
1350 North Main Street, Ann Arbor, MI. 48107
www.cushing-malloy.com

Distributed by Small Press Distribution
1341 Seventh Street, Berkeley, Ca. 94710
www.spdbooks.org

This book funded in part by The Black Diaspora Publication Fund provided by the Coleman A Young Foundation for the Department of Africana Sudies, Wayne State University.

Cover art by Maya Wynn Boyd
Cover design by Deborah King
Photo of author by Marilyn Zimmerman

ISBN 978-0-615-31290-3
Library of Congress Control Number: 2009935533

For my aunts, Virginia Boyd Bailey and Lizzie Mae Adams; my grandsons, John Percy Boyd IV and Kyler Vanderburg; my grandniece, Mya Petticord and my grandnephew, Shane Maurice Allen.

CONTENTS

Why I Observe the Sabbath at Home in the "D"

The slow kill is
a ruthless dirge
bestowed on children
beveled in star spangled
irreligious wars
over oil or vanishing
sweet waters
while political thugs
betray language
by hiding behind skin
tone and trickery of
vindictive Republicans
and nonliterary
news announcers
choking on gasoline
fumes gulping the
Gulf of Mexico
as drug dealers in
disguise sneaking
across border lines
not to pick
oranges or tobacco
or strawberries fields
laden with pesticides
of transient cancers
or corn genetically
grown for lactating
breasts of chickens
and teenagers
breeding like livestock
criminalized at birth
to fit the description
as by-products for
the prison industry or
hypnosis by X-boxes,
romance gangsta songs
and infractions of
demented movie stars

who never visit the
dark side of Detroit,
Newark, Cleveland or
Spanish-speaking
Chicago or L.A. or
any urban reservation
where desperation
breeds athletes
for battlefields
as 2-D distractions
if they can duck
that bullet shot
below the hoop
across playground
perimeters,
a hit meant
for Antoyne,
DeAndre's cousin
who spells his name
with a "y"
to make him feel special
when his mama calls
his name before
an incidental
insult of vocabulary
incites someone's
paranoid, frenetic,
delusional child
toting an automatic
to celebrate himself
on TV's "First 48"
while his parents
disappear inside
super-sized churches
hoisting misery
like pagan sacrifices
for gilded prophets
sporting blue,

alligator shoes
and gold-toothed
grins that glitter
when abusing
the Bible,
misquoting Matthew,
Mark, Luke, John,
and the Apostle Paul,
dancing preachers
dredging up testaments
condemning material
enslavement and
promising life
after Jesus' death
paid for in platinum
offering plates sucking
juice out the side
of bent necks
of faithful flocks
to put premium gas
in luxury convertibles
with chrome hub caps
spinning in reverse
in sync with wall street
investors confiscating
cityscapes by burning
houses on Halloween eve,
disabling maple trees,
ravaging evergreens,
damning rivers,
offending any
semblance of
justice until
memories curdle
in shadows of
premature death
and black streaks
of light appear

on tombstones
like hieroglyphic
tattoos encrypting
mortal damnation.

A BLACK IRON POT
In the Aftermath of Hurricane Katrina (August 2005)

Below toxic mold
and stench of rot,
beneath water stains
the color of burnt coffee grinds,
behind lines of contaminated
refrigerators gagged and bound
with duct tape and marshaled
through streets like hostages
to be hauled to burial grounds,
men in masks with mud on their shoes
claim the remains of Katrina,
as spirits imbibe
the hurricane
in a black
iron
pot.

Caught in the undertow
of Congo Square,
these histories cannot
be buried in cemeteries
at intersections of
colonial cross routes
speaking French, English,
Spanish, Patois and Chinese
in a mercenary melding port
shipping cotton, tobacco
and sugar cane;
trading corn, rum, silk,
indentured servants
and African slaves;
like ghost ships crashing
into barrier reefs haunted
by a conspiracy of greed,
New Orleans is an
imbalanced costal equation
cursed by global warnings,
vanquished people,
and forced territories.

The French Quarter
is its purgatory,
where feral cats
strut on Bourbon Street
in a vortex of sweat
and humidity
through gutters
rancid with vomit and
rank with stale alcohol,
a national house party
groaning in the gut
to Delta's blackened blues;
erupting beside Louie's
trumpet in the afterbirth
of religious abstinence
and gluttonous,
sensuous excess,
seeking magic in turquoise
beaded feathers of shamans
mapping veins in
anxious palms searching
corridors for the ghost
of Marie Leveau in red/
orange calico scarves,
scrambling tarot cards
and chicken bones,
charming Shango and
praying to river gods.

The soul of the city
lives in Creole gumbo,
in dirty rice and
Cajun cat fish fried
in the Ninth Ward,
in aesthetic communion
bent toward light
in the poetry of Dent
or invoked in Lorenzo's

eclectic, jazz phrasing
celebrating life
at a wake,
a festival of funerals
for cadavers sunken
beneath centuries of
southern terror and
murderous drownings
in the Flood of '27,
when the levee
was blown
and blacks
were sacrificed
to save wealthy whites
from a rising river,
the mighty Mississippi,
hauling the weight
of history
written in mud
and salt.

New Orleans is
a transatlantic holocaust;
bloated bodies floating
on ether between shadows
of suffocated survivors
abandoned in the fury
of nature's reclamation;
damned in a dome
and an abyss
of a whimsical President,
scratching his numb head
with disingenuous guilt
about another disastrous gulf
and prospective contracts-
the hell-of-burden
with thousands moaning
like Africans in the hull

of a slave ship cast
in a fiendish plot
in the middle
of the Atlantic
Ocean.

New Orleans is
a funeral song
hung on veils
of Spanish moss;
voices humming
in heavenly kitchens,
scaling recipes rising
above a toxic planet,
releasing necks snapped
by the rope of old
Jim Crow hiding
behind brown stained
water lines.

Lyrics forge notes
on rotting floorboards.
a choir walks
on water and song
swallows a
swollen gulf-
grieving for
New Orleans,
simmering
inside a
black
iron
pot.

Eulogy for Julia C. Collins

(18?? -1865)
Speculations on Her Thoughts in Oswego,
New York at Lake Ontario circa January 1865

Icy winds slash the waves of Lake Ontario,
dash open the wings of my winter cape
and rustle the furrows of my woolen skirt;
I invite this assault, inhale deeply to force
the frigid air into the recesses of my chest,
attempts to stifle this wretched disease,
sucking my breath, consuming my lungs
and my last winter season.

Under gray skies of hibernation,
I battle the white skeleton of death.
Like my pen pursuing the novel and this epistle,
I chase the morning light, anticipate stoic blue firs
and pliant white birch trees emitting oxygen.
The fresh crisp air soothes my raspy throat and
accentuates the paradox of a cough that intensifies
when I exhale, urgently thirsting for the next moment.
Invigorated by the immensity of vast waters
reaching infinitely for the granite coastline,
I anxiously await each, breathtaking sunset.

Unlike my fate, the heroine of my novel
does not greet death. Claire survives in the
dreams of Juno, her loyal nanny, reunites with
her father, and reconciles a broken family.
In the vista of romanticism, the white dynasty
frees the slaves, the New Orleans aristocracy
returns to their native France;
the enchanted Count marries his beloved Claire,
and then enlists with abolitionists
to make a nation free for democracy.

But before this improbable ending congealed,
the cock crowed three times at my front door.
The paper remains blank and white,
and black ink does not exonerate the slave bride,

redeem the villains, or the characters who condemned
her daughter and invented her caste.

Claire's destiny splinters into speculation
within a thousand imaginations,
then dies inaudibly in the annals of lost literatures–
taciturn tales about miscegenation in fractured families,
where mulatto children are hidden and betrayed,
veiled portraits banish relatives,
cruel patriarchs lord over estates,
and jealous, alabaster cousins serve tea
on silver trays in the shade of verandas
and fortunes supported by the injustice of
shadowy clusters of servants suffering amid
common truths and racial fictions while
they iron shirts for the master's costume,
starched cotton bosoms of opulence–
glossy, stiff, and corpulent.

In the foreground of this novel,
a nation split by contrived borders bleeds.
This war breaks brothers and breeds boys
into men marked by uniforms to draw blood
and *the dead weight of another man's ideas.*

The golden sands sift, swiftly arching toward
a noble purpose and a goal worthy of death,
perhaps for my children's children for a
grander doctrine that endows them with
respect of citizenship without the advantage
of inheritance or marriage, when daughters
can express the pleasure of intellect without
persecution from priests afraid that the body
of Mary was more than a vessel for Christ;
that she taught her Son to think with faith,
to desire beyond flesh in a world that brands
skin at birth, blinds minds with educated
wickedness, and harnesses muscles with labor
to profit and to prejudice them by.

In the masonry of God's infinite domain,
the architecture of history will construct
a new age of enlightenment with fresh influences
and new truths that embellish liberated minds.
Our paths must not *vanish in the morning mists*
that mantle the gliding stream; as workers
in the field of life we must live in earnest,
fruitions made real and resonant with freedom.

Canadian winds haul Lake Ontario
against a jagged shoreline,
cleaning waste of all matters and all creatures,
enveloping ships and sailors like salmon and trout
caught in sweeping nets without consideration
for breeds or politics. I enjoin this symphonic
progression as the moon balances the seas,
and celestial constellations enhance the sun,
as it maps the underground with vision unbound
by laws of man; like power that pilots the flight
of the phoenix, refracting prisms of light in
the wings of a dragonfly, gliding along the coast
in the clear calm after the storm.

MISS ODESSA
Odessa Wynn Brown (1923-2004)

From her front porch
she purveys politics
and urban folktales;
with sweet cakes and
coffee brewed in
a dented pot,
she ministers
the distraught
and listens
to gossip
like a TV
soap opera.

Her house is
an open door–
a nursery where
children play,
a haven where
homeless stay,
a clinic for
healing the sick–
a rest home,
where the
dying lay.

Nothing escapes
Miss Odessa's gaze–
not the discrete
swaying of trees,
nor a broken
tea leaf,
not the irregular
schedule
of the postman,
nor the scurry
of clocked workers,
not the conspiracy
of spiders

weaving traps
between cracks,
like the anonymous
assassins that
murdered
her son.

But the surgeon
could not capture
or cut out
the cancerous
creature that
found her
watching over
Strathmoor Street.

The doctors
could only offer
the balm of
narcotic sleep
to stay
the suffering
of dreams.

STAGE: BLACK

> *"Death is just the gateway to everlasting life. And change*
> *is the gateway to re-order, re-birth, renewal. To re-life."*
> —Ron Milner (1938-2004)

I first met
you in a play,
peering inside
the mind
of the character
Linda lamenting
with Smokey
Robinson's
romantic croon–
"more love,
more love"–
a scene scripted
to a Motown tune.

You could not
stay away
from this city
of automobiles,
of sweet-smoked-
barbeque-jazz,
of fried-chicken-
rhythm and blues,
of tree-lined streets
reaching as deep
as Black Bottom
and as far way
as Paradise Valley.

As a sorcerer
of words
your plays
reversed the
language of hate,
dispelled the
illusions of a
curse cast in 1943
at the barricades

when savage
rumors were
thrown off
the Belle Isle Bridge;
or in '67
on Twelfth St.
when we rebelled
against the brutality
of blind police;
or in 1972
when we exposed
homicidal under-
cover cops.

You reanimate
our chorus,
reinsert song
into monologues,
direct checkmates,
pivoting on jazz
sets salvaging
joy diminished
in the throes
of turmoil
ciphered through
the vise of the
Republic's
manifold.

Like the death dance
of a butterfly,
your writing maps
muted beauty
like pain reading
grieving flesh,
defining the gray,
creasing the lines
connecting
our past.

But like a breeze
off the Detroit River,
your passing
is rebirth,
reliving filling
this air,
this city,
as you reorder
this script,
rearrange
this scene,
determine
this set.

Stage: Black

LIKE RAIN PIERCING METAL
Sekou Sundiata (1948-2007)

Rescaling whirlwinds
of the furious '60s,
Sekou untangles
blind patriots huddled
in the eclipse of 9/11–
the white harvest
of a national
nightmare.

Sekou's sonic
treble vibrates
mind-fields of
beleaguered eagles,
breathing life
into dreams
retreating to
the 51st parallel,
beckoning citizens
to resist the heresy
of hatred and
a deadly military.

A falsetto fire bird
transposes a concert
of poets as
Sekou inscribes
this fifth season
into seven,
distinct,
unseen
languages,
like rain
piercing
metal.

WE WEEP WITH FAITH
Vivian Randall (1923-2005)

You restore rocks
from four continents,
polish each
with a diamond
needle to refract
gem stones as
smooth as
poems your
husband crafts
beneath
a crescent
moon.

You chisel earth
from veins of
antiquity,
patiently balance
a marriage
challenged by
genius and
artistic madness
fractured into
stain glass
portraits
like misshapen
clients you
stabilize with
simple pride
and some com-
prehension of
unjust pain
inflicted by
faceless men
with intellects
of shellfish
and flaccid
hands beyond
their reach.

26

In gray seasons
we weep
with faith,
dust diminishes
human flesh,
and alpha women
assume power
embedded in stone.

PHOENIX RISING

Mayor Coleman Alexander Young (1918-1997)
"Cities have died, have burned, yet phoenix-like returned"
-Dudley Randall

Immersed in
Detroit/Alabama,
Black-Bottom blues,
automobile plants,
union organizing,
and lush life imaginings
in syncopated swing
inspired in Paradise Valley,
the irascible Coleman
Alexander Young
was reborn in the ashes
of freedom battles.

Capitalist police
harassed him
and sabotaged
his name;
a segregated
military clipped
his eagle wings
and grounded
this Tuskegee airman;
FBI spies invaded
his privacy and
blacklisted him
as a communist red,
like Paul Robeson
and Richard Wright,
Langston Hughes,
Lorraine Hansberry,
and Dr. Martin Luther King–
free-thinking,
articulate descendants
of literate ex-slaves.

With bravado and
an audacious vocabulary

Coleman exposed the
Un-American motives
of Senator McCarthy's
sinister committee,
deconstructed this skullduggery
and conspiracies to stop
crusades to make freedom real,
even if it only existed
in dreams within the radius
of Detroit city limits,
in the "arsenal of democracy,"
where the UAW and
community elders debated
politics with haircuts in
barbershops for young men
intended to topple pyramids
of unjust hierarchies
constructed over four centuries.

"Black and White together,"
Coleman chimed in unison
when Detroit elected him
to end police terrorism;
this mayor rebuked
suburban antipathy
damning the dark city
and its brazen leader—
a raconteur often seen
retelling stories with
factory workers on
street corners, or
carousing after hours
with radicals convening
in beer taverns, or
reciting an elegy in
the bitter-sweet sanctity
of a funeral rite of passage.

Republicans tried
to banish him;
obsessed Federal
agencies armed with
legal daggers
plotted to arrest him;
with poison ink and
jaundiced headlines
newspaper editors
deemed to defame him;
but for 20 years
the citizens voted
for the tenacious,
charismatic Coleman,
a phoenix rising from
the white ashes of
freedom clashes.

DANCING IS FLYING
Jackie Hilsman (1936-2002)

Dancing is flying,
dancing is flying
on top of your father's
swing-tipped steps,
lifting you
unto riffs
in Ellington's
winged
symphonics.

Dancing is flying,
dancing is flying
with a pistol
in your purse
tight to the hip
behind the
steel door
of your studio
where bare feet
reach for cusps
of hope deleting
despair,
greeting art
liberating air
empowered by
sheer leotard
bodies leaping
higher than tragic
reflex spawned
like trash thrown
from distorted
grimaces of
pale masks.

Dancing is flying,
dancing is flying
in experimental
movements above
submissive sterility
and a society
of gravity
and disease
that crippled
your leg
but could not
break the swing
of your winged
steps dancing,
is flying
is dancing
is flying
is dancing
is flying
is
dancing
is
flying
is
dancing
is

A HAND PAINTED DESERT
Lorenzo Thomas (1944-2005)

Lorenzo,
your poetry
is my touchstone,
where I brace
breath when
weakened by
imperialist terror
inciting lies
behind towers
of clay, mining
cold hysterics
from unforgivable
intrigue.

You inspire my
dissident vocabulary
with intellectual spirit
found in poems
we deliver in
Paris, Liverpool,
Italy and Spain,
worlds translated
into German
in Osnabrück
for audiences
in Müenster,
poetry too often
ignored by councils
of scholars in
our own country
where your charm
tolerated my
rebellious outbursts
at the sight of
stiff paradigms
choking poems

as critical assassins
bludgeon literary
icons with impunity
in New Orleans,
New York, Baltimore,
Chicago and in books
buried with encryptions
with no jazz.

It was your
gracious strength
and sense of humor
in spite of the spite
conspiring to
hush knowledge
in your relentless
pen that disquieted
their discourteous
discourse even
when audiences
were thin with
recognition.

It was a great time
to be poets,
and I give these
clips to recollect
the physics
of memory as
I hold dear
in this image
of you writing
inside a hand
painted desert,
reconsidering a
black thunder cloud
and the promise
of rain.

REARRANGING YOUR FATHER'S TABLE
Manning Marable (1950-2011)

"Before I die,
I want to write
a box full of books,"
you said, and this
image becomes
a catalogue
inside my head
as years transpose
sites for industry
and I collect
your words
in my library,
and share in
your endeavor
while the viscissitudes
of intellect and tendons
of acedemic politics
mirror your visage
like Frederick Douglass'.

It is the night
your twins are born,
Sojourner and Joshua,
and so we talk
about legacies
and uncertainties,
like the challenge of
investigating race
and democracies
conflicted by class.

We exchange quotes
from Marx and Ida B.;
Frances Harper talks
back to Booker T.
as we reshape declining
unions in deserted factories,
and re-imagine revolutionary
fields in Cuba with Ché

and Guillén then
transpose Dudley
Randall's poetry
with Diégo Rivera's
mural inside a
Detroit Museum.

II.

Enroute to Paris,
I hear of your death.
my flight is laden
with grief.
a carrier pigeon
observes me from
the hotel window.
a feather appears
on my sunken pillow.

I visit the crypt
of Aimé Cesaire.
bells toll across
Luxembourg Garden
and tulips convene
in the passing
of eternal promises
reported in
Sojourner's psalms
when we are again
led into battle
by Joshua.

I visit you in the
dream realm of
the afterlife,
where symbols
are configured
and warnings
are encoded
for the living.

You are busy
in the offices
of history.
your silver hair
entangles blue
space like the
mane of Douglass,
as you stroke
your chin
like Malcolm
seated next
to DuBois.

You are home,
rearranging your
Father's table.

SOFT WHITE PEARLS
Inez Boyd Foston (1897-2002)

A veritable
attorney
of words,
a dictionary
of deportment,
a surveyor
of precision
in declension
sent to light
libraries,
you are
like the soft
white pearls
you adorn,
an infinitely,
balanced
valence,
teaching
symmetrical
passages to
generations
of classes,
decoding
messages
beyond
the delta
into the
magnificence
of unwritten
diasporas.

FEARLESS BEAUTY
Willa Beatrice Boyd Gaston (1906-2007)

An Amerindian offspring
fused from Jewish-African,
mulatto veins,
you are testament
to a tradition that never
bowed or scraped
to ingratiate myths
assigned by benefactors
of Alabama slave masters.

Perhaps the descendant
of a vibrant and regal
Senegalese maiden
kidnapped by the waterfall
when her father
was not watching,
you are the last
and the first
of seven generations
since emancipation.

From the beginning,
your meticulous mother,
well-known as Selma's
finest *modiste*,
designed your dresses
in Parisian fashions,
and like a queen,
delineating cultural
aesthetics on college campuses,
you claimed your crown,
ignited power from charm,
married a man made of legends,
and mothered a daughter
who would invent futures
from unfinished kingdoms.

You held court in classrooms,
instilling finesse, sensibility
and intelligence in children
constrained by the inequities of
the color line reflected in the
double consciousness of
distorted mirrors.

In the shattered aftermath
of your husband's irreconcilable
decision, you renewed life
with daughter Alice
in the wonderland of
grandchildren inside your
son-in-law's protective enclave,
and then took flight,
circling continents and oceans,
flashing star dust inside medieval
castles and ancient pyramids;
stepping on sandstones
approaching dusty pillars,
where philosophers cloistered
and prophets hesitated
to investigate mistakes
and console our humanity.

But now,
in full view of
holiday lights
and timelessness,
your descendants
contemplate your
centennial and marvel
at your fearless beauty–
that always arrives
wearing a dazzling smile
and the most stunning,
stylish fashion.

By Self Election-L'Raison D'Être
Alma Young (1947-2004)

I'll miss promises
to lunch at the
neighborhood café
on the next Saturday
or to take tea
in sunlit gardens
in spring moments
lost under a
deluge of papers,
committees,
symposiums,
dissertations,
or conferences
as you balance
a mélange of
scholarly dialogues,
mental equations
deduced with
officious precision
before speckled
audiences.

In the absence
of missed retreats,
we steal time
in our offices
to rejoice in our
laurels as mothers,
to shed our adult
disguises in academic
regalia, giggling like
teenage girls on the
telephone as we unveil
daggers of adversity
encoded in odious
verbosity that rattles
with dim humor
in green rooms
with dull light.

In a hostile
demography
mediated by
intellectual
imperialism
and a fear
of blackness,
you resist
contentious forces
with quiet valor
born of an ancient
womb,
and when our
voices touch,
the sky feels
free to breathe
by self election,
l'raison d'être-
as activists
of intellect,
as black,
as woman,
you walk
in subtle,
defiant form.

C'EST UNE HISTOIRE EXTRAORDINAIRE
for Michel and Geneviève Fabre

We escape
to *Paris*
to liberate
the American
dictionary,
to write
ourselves out
of metaphors
cursing the color
of expatriate
authors estranged
from our native
tongue.

And you are
ambassadors
on journeys
to foreign
literature,
harboring
inscriptions
of black aesthetics
condemned for
angry cadence
yearning to speak
as freely as bebop
transcending grief
making love
by *le Seine*
when the spring
of '68
merged centuries
of revolutions
convening with
Negritude to
celebrate Josephine's
magnificent derrière

and Ellington's
luminous suites.

You contradict
snide dismissals
of Wright's Bigger,
you explicate
reasoning for
violent imagery
distilled into
poetic beauty,
and theorize
that masking
is coded magic
in plays like
Sidney Bechet's
vertical schematics
romancing your
affection into
marriage,
while you reveal
mystery within
our subversive
imaginary of
nouveau noire
protest
art.

We escape
to *Paris*,
and you are
our embassy;
c'est une histoire
extraordinaire.

BLOODHOUNDS ON MY TRAIL
Ode to Kathryne

In the summer of 1943,
a race riot exploded
in the "Arsenal
of Democracy"
when two rumors said
a woman and her baby
were hurled off
the MacArthur Bridge,
cast into the
violent undertow
of the Detroit riverbed.

The white story said
a black man did it;
blacks reported
a white man
was seen at the
scene of the crime.

Twisted gossip
whet appetites,
and bent voracious
ears by inverting
skin tones to match
conflicted witnesses.

No bodies
were recovered,
except those
lining the morgue
after attacks on
curious citizens
enticed by an
unsolved mystery
to a never ending
flow of trouble.

Kathryne's MacArthur
Bridge is a General

kicking fascist ass
and freeing prisoners
chained to barbed
wire war camps.

Kathryne's MacArthur
Bridge is the overture
in a Beatles' song,
where hippies commune,
and protest for peace
while passing a joint
and dancing barefoot
in the grass.

In 1991, Kathryne
adopted the woes
of this city,
left Harvard
to teach racial
justice at an urban
university in
language that clotted
conversations with
broken arrows and
scattered feathers,
like Chief Tecumseh
defending the
Great Lakes in
the War of 1812.

Ezra Pound and
T.S. Eliot cannot
understand her affection
for Langston Hughes
and his Harlem Renaissance,
or her interest in the
League of Revolutionary
Black Workers,
or why she debates

the gatekeepers of
the King's English
in favor of proletarian
citizens speaking
in the cadence
of Hitsville lyrics.

What congeals in
her twinkling eye
while lingering too near
incurable colleagues
or pondering a malaise
of entangled theories,
or figuring a mystery
at an overpass
linking this life
to timelessness–
is a tiny fissure
of doubt,
an opening for
an uninvited visitor
who intervenes during
a fragile pause
in the library,
whose prodding
for attention
disrupts her
articulating pen,
trips her thoughts
and deletes brilliant
phrases from
finely crafted,
agonizing passages.

When Kathryne
turns her head,
he teases her cats
and chases them

under furniture,
and when she closes
her bedroom door,
this hairless
creature with
translucent skin
reappears just
above her head
to vent about irrelevant,
intellectual endeavors,
to mock her passions
and her affiliations
with persons of
marginal status
to the detriment
of her talents.

He drinks her beer
and gives her cigarettes
in the dark of night.
he erases her
phone messages,
interrupts conversations
with her dead husband,
and convinces her
no one knows that
the secret to this
conundrum is hidden
under a snow-covered
ledge of the
MacArthur Bridge,
and he promises
answers will be
revealed after
the winter storm
covers their tracks
and conceals her
human scent.

He sits on the
steel railing,
sneering at her.
this skinny,
naked haunt laughs
as she claws
through freshly
fallen snow,
and sifts through
mounds of rock salt
for some sign,
for some clue
only he knew.

In a rush of disgust,
Kathryne grabs the
ghost and chokes
his bony throat, but
his talking continues,
his tongue hanging
over the right side
of his mouth, drooling
while accusing her
of conducting bourgeois,
erudite research.

He hurls cruel lies
about her closest friends,
exclaims how hopeless
love is and how
no one reads great
literature anymore
than they care about
workers' rights
or the invisibility
of dark people
residing in incessant
poverty in a history

blinded by headlights
and certain oblivion.

She snaps his neck,
and in that instant
he vanishes and
a shadowy figure
of a faceless,
raceless woman,
as pale as Kathryne's
Norwegian grand-
mother appears,
cradling a baby
as brown and
as smooth as
casings of freshly
fallen chestnuts.

Suddenly, the
creature reconfigures
on the opposite side
of the bridge,
holding his broken
neck upright between
his bony fingers,
shouting:

> "Yeah, I did it.
> Right here,
> from this very spot.
> Talked her into a frenzy.
> Told her they would
> kill her and that
> blasphemous infant,
> and you can't save them,
> and you can't change them."

Mother and child fall,
spiraling in the fury
of the squall.
Kathryne follows,
floating downward
as a cacophony of
raging sounds
encircle them.

Like the snow storm
halting traffic
and cleansing
city streets,
three bodies part
the frozen river,
and maddening
echoes stop.

WITHOUT FEAR OR HATRED
Dr. David C. Northcross, Jr. (1917-2009)

Physicians deliver life,
arrest bleeding,
repair bones,
mend broken skin,
intercept disease
and predict the end,
even in the dark of night,
in the shadow of fright
cast by a burning,
sacrilegious cross,
forcing them
to flee North,
to build homes
and hospitals.

David Northcross, Jr.
is born into a covenant
to medicine without pretense
within hallowed walls
of his parent's clinic,
and he does not squint in
the white glare of incivility,
nor does he adhere to impressions
of racist supremacy in universities
or in a segregated army.

The genius of swing
rejuvenates him at
nightclub recitals,
irreconcilable blues
heals him after
marital fractures,
and despite the acerbity
of measured, parental
affection, his children
flourish in this DNA,
exploring the dense
thickets of hostility

in a terrain where
prejudice lingers
behind soiled sheets,
fearing scientific logic
and diminishing capacity
to enforce false privilege.

He travels the planet,
and checks into
exclusive residences,
hotels where brown people
clean, serve, and cook
while he secures visas
for black physician
conventions,
and skies along
the coasts of Brazil
and Acapulco.

Dr. David C. Northcross, Jr.
rebuked unnatural deaths,
envisioned his own time,
claimed his own pace
and upheld a sacred trust
that humans should live fully
without fear of blood or hatred
that threatens the dark.

WORKING IT OUT

Kenn Cox (1940-2008)
"A lot of people have died for this music," –Dizzy Gillespie

Black keys
conversing
with ivory
like oblique
irony in
unrhymed
psalms

Chopin sonatas
confer with
Strayhorn symphonics
Monk disrupts
with tempos
linked like dominoes

this dialogue occurs
with Kenn Cox
composing suites
on piano
without primacy
in *Multidirection*
or as *Guerrilla Jams*
engaging a
dystrophic democracy

on dim streets
blue notes
stud starlight
at high altitudes

Kenn Cox
at the keys
channeling ebony
freely through
the integrity
of well-honed
ivory

A MINGUS AMONG US AND A WALDEN WITHIN US
Donald Walden (1938-2008)

Dexter Gordon
glances back,
sees Donald Walden
taking Giant Steps
in clear, fluid space.

So, Dexter holds the gate,
makin' the jazz greats wait–
Monk, Bird, Coltrane,
the contentious Miles,
the tumultuous Lateef
and the sultry Billie–
makin' a wake
for the sax man
from Detroit
by way of
St. Louie,
representin' bebop
breaking fixed notes,
traversing linear scales,
and all repressive
constrictions impaled
on music sheets,
resisting the
inconvenience
of mortal skin
when spirit enchants
song and rules of
Earth bound
dominions
diminish.

In the "D"
we call him
"the bebop police,"
who styles in
razor sharp,
GQ slacks
as distinctive
as his tenor sax,
articulating
transformative
sets marking
planets.

Yeah,
there is a
Mingus
among us,
but there is
a Donald Walden
within us.

CRYSTALLIZING THE MOON
Mick Vranich (1946-2010)

When the blues
follows your steps,
poetry lines are
as deliberate as
a union washing
blood off a contract,
measurements
as foreboding
as the howl of
bloodhounds tracking
radicals like criminals
stealing freedom
after midnight.

Mick could find a lilt
in this pathos,
could rock a poem
about hard knocks
in Detroit
like a siren protesting
murdered dreams.

It's like listening
to guitar hymns
resonating on
the underbelly
of saxophones
soaked in funky
beer notes
rising above the
Cass Corridor.

Or like watching
the blues
crystallizing
the moon.

PURPLE HAZE FOR RONNIE
Harry "Ronnie" Smith (1960-2010)

Mothers should not
bury sons.
daughters should not
lose fathers before
becoming women.

But sun can
shine through rain
and each life
carries its
own clock.

Ronnie rocks time
with arched smiles
hitched to the wings
of Jimmy Hendrix's
guitar strings.

He videos us
in reunion,
recording laughter,
lies and family lore
for listening
ancestors,
freezing space
connecting cities,
and states to
a Jamaican bay.

When it's raining
and the sun's shining,
Old Africans say,
the devil is beating
his wife.

Ronnie would say,
there's a party
on the horizon,
making purple haze
while we kiss the sky.

COVENANT OF CONTRADICTORY FORCES
for Mildred Wynn Varner

I've been told
she is the daughter
where a father
imprinted his soul—
that when he
touched her cheek,
a covenant of
contradictory forces
shook hands and
converged in
opposite corners.

She is a paradox.
genuine warmth strapped
with a soothsayer's sword.
she is the embodiment
of uncompromised
honesty heightened
with the temperament
of an avenging angel
on an unappreciated,
but clearly defined
mission.

She is the teacher who
grades the final test.
she is the bitter–sweet
voice of revelations
that fights the devil
and argues for your
last chance without
taking a breath.

She is a tall glass
of water from
the fountain of
redemption

who provides
fruit from her
abundance and
serves it on a
gold-rimmed
plate and satin
trimmed linen.

She is her father's
unfaltering faith.
she is the
confluence
of steadfast
convictions,
the painful
resolution
of grace.

SIGHT UN-SCENE
at Sundance

Eyes wide
with desire
to occupy
your light
to steal beauty
from a celluloid
reflection that
feigns audiences
with this neurosis:

film script scenarios
flash your flawless,
dimpled smile
women crave
insatiably as you
move through danger
with bravado other
men fail to imitate
by tilting their
bobbing heads.

And fans applaud
your starlit name
as the romantic heroic
who does not falter
or suffer visible
acne scars like
the disparagingly
ordinary who
envy the illusion,
the fantasy,
the sexual
glory.

Sight un-scene,
a subplot to
assassinate
perfection
develops—
cold and naked,
quaking in
surreal lens
of pretend,
imagery shatters—
death by drugs,
or an alcoholic
drowning,

or, you plummet
into an abyss
after a disastrous,
fiery scandal—
whatever purges
idolatry of the
unholy.

MAPLE RED

A poetic interlude with the painting by Edward Clark

Tangerine swelling with
sanguine sea foam
like Indigo blues,

the measure of
the weight of gravity
fusing into twilight–

the mellowing of
antagonisms
into yesteryears,
imprinting the primacy
of maple red.

This Small Opening

When the tide
reaches the
beach,
it doesn't
matter which
wave brought
this small
opening when
we touched
slightly,
deliberately,
despite the
inconvenience
of the hour.

Tension sustains.
it doesn't unravel
when sea recedes
into dawn.

Whatever occurs
returns as naturally
as waves chasing
the mood of the
moon.

No One is Innocent, But

No one is innocent,
and in some ways
we are all guilty—
guilty in our selfishness,
guilty in our wastefulness,
guilty in our impotent,
paralyzed ignorance.

But, some of us
are more guilty—
guilty in their
corporate corruption,
guilty in their
power trippin'
and playa hatin',
guilty in their
lyin' to the poor,
guilty in their
cuttin' taxes
for the wealthy,
protectin' their
excessive possessions
and their psychopathic,
diversionary war.

No one is innocent, but
we damn well know
that an impostor
executed daddy's
vendetta, that
his brother
dumped ballots
in the Atlantic Ocean,
that this perpetratin'
president stole
the national election,

that his dim-witted
wife banished
peace poetry from
the undemocratic,
de-constitionalized,
White House mansion.

No one is innocent, but
we know the same
illiterate stooge,
who nearly flunked
out of Yale University,
got into Harvard Law School
claiming his upper class
Texas perspective
satisfied cultural diversity.
this same guilty party
was dissin' affirmative action.

Tell me George W,
is there a 10% quota
for African Americans
drafted and killed
in action?

In a Pluto Republic
platitudes and slogans
pledge patriotism
and allegiance to war,
and the language
of poets is banished
from the court.

Like warm rain
in February
our words form
puddles in bookstores
and libraries.
we sing white
spaces into carrier
codes illuminated by
the black ink of
knowing fear
breeds in
deaf shadows
and bends the
human spine
until the backbone
snaps!

Our poems
are stained
documentaries
of life after
death,
resolute
warnings
spun from
blinding
crosswinds.

The beauty is
this metaphor
can't be bought:

poetry rising
on sunbeams
returns as
raindrops
in the desert
of Iraq.

WRITTEN IN INVISIBLE INK
for Ollie

"It's not personal," he said.
but the agenda written
in invisible ink read:

> It is privilege.
> It is fraternity.
> It is tradition.
> It is a rejection
> contrived by
> aspersions
> to maintain
> power beyond
> suspect.

Silence is complicit,
denial informs repression,
and arrogance infects participants,
retreating to the first lie told
to discolor your mother's name,
to drag America's integrity
down through the bowels
of a slave ship hole.

Abstract assaults by
committee are insidious,
systemic, paradoxical,
practices of persons
against persons,
which is very
personal.

SWIMMING WITH GAPING WAVES
D.O.G. (2000-2007)

My son John bought
you for 50 dollars
from a dope addict
at a gas station
near a freeway exit–
saves you from
abusive fate
that befalls large dogs
guarding homes
terrorized by crime.

D.O.G. found elegant
sound enunciated through
demeanor: "Diogi,"
a black and tan
Rottweiler who
sports a luxurious
coat and travels with
a silver suit case.

You go to university
and learn compound sounds,
pout like a queen
when ignored and
sulk like a spoiled child
when scolded for being
a dog digging up tulip bulbs.

You vacation in Tobermory,
the Grand Dame of the Georgian Bay,
swimming with gaping waves,
circling our frigid bodies,
warding us away
from the dangerous
undertow of the strait
or the slithering path
of water snakes.

You never bark
at rabbits or growl
at squirrels that
catch your gaze,
but chase them
merrily along trails
that lead you astray
along the lake
or into the city,
where you never
raise your alarm
at women or children,
only strange men
glancing askance
as they pass
our gate.

Then, in a swift,
elusive moment,
disease intrudes
and ends your
last season.
and while we weep
like children
afraid of the night,
seven Canadian
geese wait
for you under
a street lamp
outside the
hospital
to guide your
final adventure,
to coast along
the eastern
shoreline of
Lake Huron.

LOVE REALIZES
for Charles and Sandra on their Wedding Day

Charles collects
black and white
photographs,
reframes forgotten
prints retrieved
from riots,
from fires frozen
into ashen pasts,
like tree roots
reaching for
earth and oxygen.

He simmers a
serene fierceness
friends visit
seeking common
sense and even
smiles that often
elude intellectuals
and activists as they
swear about sellout
politicians bleeding
profits from vacant lots,
just beyond the
front porch
of Charles' house.

Sandra collects
stories from books,
unveiling tropes
effacing similes
and silk linings
reinforcing metaphors.

She sees Charles
contouring nephews
into erect men,

recasting neighbor-
hoods with vital
biographies to
sustain an
indefinite city
succumbing to
fallen leaves
in a cold,
dry season.

In this disquieting
texture of restorations,
love recognizes
Charles and Sandra
Simmons
realized.

WE WANT OUR CITY BACK

We want our city back.
We want our streetlights on.
We want our garbage gone.
We want our children
playing on playgrounds,
but not with loaded guns.
We want to retire
by the river
and raise collard greens
in abandoned fields.
We want our ancestors
to rest in peace.
We want our city back.

We don't want law and order.
We want justice and jobs.
We don't want small business.
We mean serious business.
No more Mom and Pop wig shops.
No more Mickey D's
rappin' with the homies.
No more Dollar Stores
We need groceries.
No more Dixie Colonels
serving Kente cloth cuisine.
No more taco supreme.
No more indigestion or
quick-fix politics.
We want our city back.

We don't want police
harassing the homeless
for being without a lease.
We don't want video cops
bustin' crack heads
with flashlights at night.
We want peacekeepers
to capture the real dope men

reclining in respectable privilege.
We want our taxes to track
down the real assassins.
We want our city back.

We don't want Euro-centric
or Afro-eccentric edu-macations.
We want a freedom curriculum.
We want a liberated vision
in history remembered.
We don't want our children
crunched like computer chips
to fit in the old world order,
worshiping slave holding
societies in Egypt or Greece.
We want the board of education
to take a lie detector test
for neglect of the intellect,
for assault on our children's senses.
We don't want them to be GM execs,
or rejects in labor camps.
We want dignity,
not cupidity.
We want our city back.

No more text-sex mess.
No more zoot-suit mayors,
shuffling skeletons and abuses
like gamblers losing pay checks.
No more ex-basketball,
suburban, bing-a-ling mayors,
ignoring inner city citizens
living next to boarded-up
doors and bolted windows.
No more broken trees.
No more motor city casinos,
or dilapidated buildings
where junkies, rodents

and vermin spring.
We want our city back.

We want the river dredged
for distraught souls.
We want our homes rebuilt.
We want the guilty
to pay a greed tax
for the living they stole.
We want our city back.

Hey! We ain't going away
like fugitives slaves
escaping to Canaday!
Our backs are up
against the wall.
This is our clarion call.
Feed the hungry.
Clothe the ragged.
Heal the sick.
Enlighten the ignorant.
Punish the wicked.
And raise the dead!

We want our streetlights on.
We want our garbage gone.
We want to be rid
of smack and crack.
We want to retire
by the river.
We want our ancestors
to rest in peace.
We are claiming our history,
seizing the hour.
Cause, we mean to take
our city back.

POETIC NOTES

Odessa (Wynn) Brown was the mother of Hayward Brown and the aunt of the author. Hayward Brown was tried and acquitted of murder and attempted murder of six Detroit police officers, who were members of the controversial, undercover unit, STRESS (Stop the Robberies, Enjoy Safe Streets). He was harassed by police until he was mysteriously murdered in 1984.

Julia C. Collins was a nineteenth century writer, who died before she completed her serialized novel, *The Curse of Caste; or, The Slave Bride,* which appeared in 1865 in *The Christian Recorder,* the publication of the African Methodist Episcopal Church. The italicized words are taken from Collins' novel and her essays. This rediscovered novel has been the subject of scholarship and has been reprinted as a book. For more information see fall 2007 issue of *The African American Review,* where this poem first appeared.

Kenn Louis Cox II was a prominent, internationally acclaimed pianist and jazz composer. Although he was born and resided in Detroit for most of his life, he traveled throughout the world and played with musicians, such as Charles McPherson, Rahsaan Roland Kirk, Kenny Burrell and Yusef Lateel, and mentored subsequent generations of musicians, such as Geri Allen, Marion Hayden and Rod William. His original compositions have been recorded by jazz greats, such as the Jazz Crusaders. His work with Detroit musicians Donald Walden and Marcus Belgrave, among many others, nourished and inspired the music scene in Detroit with creativity and spirituality.

Michel Fabre and Geneviève Fabre are French scholars known for their studies in African American literature. Michel Fabre wrote the definitive biography on Richard Wright and is considered the expert on African American expatriate writers who lived in France. Genevieve's career converges and diverges with her interest in African American women writers and Chicano(a) women writers. They were both professors at the Sorbonne for many years. Michel died on August 16, 2007.

Inez Boyd Foston graduated from Knoxville College and taught English at Tennessee State University in the 1920s. After she married, she moved Hopkinsville, Kentucky and eventually settled in Detroit at the beginning of World War II and became an principal of a Lutheran elementary school. After retirement, she taught English and Mathematics at Lewis Business College in Detroit.

Willa Beatrice Boyd Gaston was the sister of Inez Foston; both were great-aunts of the author. She was a graduate of Tennessee State University and a home economics teacher in Chattanooga, Tennessee until the suicidal death of her husband. She relocated in Detroit with her daughter and son-in-law, Alice and Dr. Julius Combs. She traveled around the world and was known for her warmth and generous friendship.

Jackie Hilsman taught dance and physical education for more than thirty years at Detroit Northern High School; and with Peter Bernard, founded Experimental Movement, a creative studio that taught modern dance and performance with black music and poetry. Their professional dance company worked with some of Detroit foremost artists, including Geri Allen, Marcus Belgrave, Kenn Cox, Dudley Randall, Melba Joyce Boyd, Ted Sheeley, and many others.

Kathryne Lindberg was a nationally acclaimed scholar and author, and was a professor at Wayne State University from 1991 until her disappearance on December 13, 2010. Originally from San Francisco, she received her PhD in English from Columbia University and taught at Harvard University before coming to Detroit. She shifted her focus from traditional research in literature to explore the contributions of unsung heroes in Detroit, who were responsible for bringing social justice to African Americans and the working class. She lived in downtown by the Detroit River.

Ron Milner was a major playwright, who lived and worked in Detroit. His award-winning plays were performed all over the country and featured actors like Ruby Dee, Glynn Turman, Denzel Washington, Ella Joyce, Paul Winfield, E. Apatha Merkeson, and many others. He was one of the founders of Concept East Theatre, the Langston Hughes Theatre and the Paul Robeson Theatre. "Black Bottom" and "Paradise Valley" were the first black communities in Detroit; 1943 the year of a Race Riot in Detroit; "'67" was the year of another major race riot in Detroit; the undercover cops were called "STRESS," a police decoy unit that systematically entrapped and murdered citizens (1971-73). (See information on Miss Odessa)

Dr. David C. Northcross, Jr. was the son of two physicians, David and Daisy Northcross, who were threatened and harassed by the Ku Klux Klan for opening a medical practice in Alabama. In 1916, they relocated to Detroit, and in 1917 they founded Mercy Hospital. When David Jr. took over management of the hospital, he expanded the hospital with a new building in 1956 that served the Black community for several decades until his retirement.

Vivian Spenser Randall was a psychiatric social worker, a world traveler and a lapidary. She was born in Lexington, Kentucky and moved to Detroit to attend Wayne State University, where she received two degrees in Social Work. She was the wife of Dudley Randall (1914-2000), the famous Detroit poet and founder of Broadside Press.

Charles and Sandra Simmons are activist scholars and educators who operate Hush House in Detroit. Charles is a professor of journalism at Eastern Michigan University and constructs traveling exhibits about African American history. Sandra teaches at Wayne State University, where she is completing a PhD in English. Together, they run "Hush House," a community project that inspires Detroit youth to aspire despite difficult times and adversity that besets their neighborhoods.

Sekou Sundiata was a native New Yorker and a renown performance poet who began writing poetry and working with musicians during the Black Arts Movement. He was a professor at the New School for Social Research. In wake of 9/11, he traveled throughout the United States, meeting with poets, advocating poetry for social uplift and progressive ideas for the redefinition of citizenship, and new meanings for the American Dream.

Lorenzo Thomas was one of the foremost poets and scholars to emerge from the Black Arts Movement. He published several books of poetry, a major book of literary criticism, and countless essays for newspapers and periodicals. He was a professor at the University of Houston. His work is internationally acclaimed.

Mildred Wynn Varner is an aunt of the author and a retired school teacher, living in Bessemer, Alabama. She is respected throughout her community as an advocate of education, racial progress and speaking the truth.

Mick Vranich was born and raised in Wyandotte, MI. After traveling in Europe, he lived for seven years in California, performing his music and poetry. After returning to Detroit he became a respected community activist, living and working throughout the city, documenting and combating cultural problems faced in everyday life. Mick combined his abilities as a carpenter, writer, musician, and organizer to address social and community issues, heading up projects that offered informative dialogue and aid to such citizen groups as area food banks, Native American justice issues and veterans' matters. Mick was the author of four books of poetry, *Salad Surreal: Discernible by Distortion* (Salad Press, Detroit 1971), *Radnik Pisar* (2X4 Press, 1983), *Boxer's Break* (Past Tents Press, 1987), and *Sawhorse* (Doorjamb Press, 1999), and six recordings of his music and poetry, from New Alliance Records in Los Angeles and Raven in Detroit. Mick and his wife, the artist Sherry Hendrick created the art gallery, Alley Culture, located in the Woodbridge Farms area of Detroit.

Donald Walden was born in St. Louis, MO, but lived the majority of his life in Detroit. He was stellar musician, who was mentored by Barry Harris and Yusef Lateef. Donald was a jazz educator at Oberlin University, and subsequently became a tenured professor at the University of Michigan in Jazz Studies. As a Motown musician, he played with several singers and musicians, including Stevie Wonder. He also played with the Queen of Soul, Aretha Franklin during this earlier period. In addition to his close collaborations with Kenn Cox, he recorded and performed nationally and internationally with Barry Harris, Roy Brooks, Charles McPherson, Lonnie Hillyer, Betty Carter, The Sun Ra Arkestra, Branford Marsalis, Tommy Flanagan, Marcus Belgrave, Rod Hicks, Marion Hayden, and many other jazz greats.

Alma Young was a professor at Wayne State University and held the Coleman A. Young Endowed Chair. In her last appointment before her death, she served as the Dean of the College of Urban, Labor and Metropolitan Affairs. Before coming to Detroit, she was a professor at the University of New Orleans and served on the Board of Commissioners for the Port of New Orleans. She received a doctorate in Political Science from Massachusetts Institute of Technology, a master's degree in Journalism from Columbia University, and bachelor's in Government and Philosophy from Radcliffe College. An internationally respected political scientist, Alma specialized in urban issues affecting people of color, women and children.

Coleman Alexander Young was the first black mayor of the City of Detroit. He was a Tuskegee Airman, a labor organizer, and was famous for his defiant stance at his hearing before Senator McCarthy House on Un-American Activities. He appointed Dudley Randall poet laureate of Detroit in 1981. The epigram at the beginning of the poem is from Randall's poem, "Detroit Renaissance," which he dedicated to Mayor Young.

ABOUT THE AUTHOR

Melba Joyce Boyd is the author of nine books of poetry, and has received many grants and awards for her poetry, including a Michigan Council for the Arts Individual Artist Award for *Song for Maya* (Broadside Press/Detroit River Press, 1983), which was also translated and published in Germany. She was commissioned to write the official poem for the Charles H. Wright Museum of African American History, which is inscribed in the museum. Lines from her poem, "We Want Our City Back," appear in the sculpture, "Transcending: Michigan's Tribute to Labor," installed in Hart Plaza in downtown Detroit. Her poetry has been published in numerous periodicals, online journals and anthologies. She often performs her poetry with jazz musicians and is currently collaborating with bassist Marion Hayden in a series of video poems.

Boyd was the assistant editor at Dudley Randall's Broadside Press (1972-77), and is the editor of *Roses and Revolutions: The Selected Writings of Dudley Randall* (Wayne State Univ. Press, 2009) which won the 2010 Independant Publishers Gold Award for Poetry, the 2010 Michigan Notable Book Award and was a finalist for both the 2010 NAACP Image Award for Poetry and the 2010 ForeWord Award for an Anthology. She is the author of *Wrestling with the Muse: Dudley Randall and the Broadside Press* (Columbia Univ. Press, 2004) which received the American Library Association Black Caucus Honor for Nonfiction.She is also the author of *Discarded Legacy: Politics and Poetics in the Life of Frances E. W. Harper, 1825-1911* (Wayne State Univ. Press, 1994) and co-editor with M.L. Liebler of *Abandon Automobile: Detroit City Poetry 2001* (Wayne State Univ. Press., 2001).

She is a Distinguished University Professor and Chair of the Department of Africana Studies at Wayne State University and an Adjunct Professor in the Department of Afroamerican and African Studies at the University of Michigan-Ann Arbor, where she received her Doctor of Arts in English (1979). She has presented her poetry and scolarship in Africa, Europe, and the Republic of China, but her life and work is based in her city of origin, Detroit, Michigan and in Tobermory, Ontario in Canada, where she spends her summers with her family.

MORE POETRY BY MELBA JOYCE BOYD

CAT EYES AND DEAD WOOD (Fallen Angel Press, 1979)
SONG FOR MAYA (Broadside Press/Detroit River Press, 1982)
THIRTEEN FROZEN FLAMINGOES (Die Certel Press, Germany, 1984)
THE INVENTORY OF BLACK ROSES (Past Tents Press, 1989)
LIED FÜR MAYA (Verlag Press, Germany, 1989)
LETTERS TO CHÉ (Ridgeway Press, 1996)
THE PROVINCE OF LITERARY CATS (Past Tents Press, 2002)
BLUES MUSIC SKY OF MOURNING: THE GERMAN POEMS (Past Tents Press, 2006)